WAYS INTO HISTORY

The Great Fire of London

Sally Hewitt

W

FRANKLIN WATTS

LONDON•SYDNEY

First published in 2004 by
Franklin Watts
338 Euston Rd
London NW1 3BH

Franklin Watts Australia
Level 17/207 Kent Street
Sydney, NSW 2000

© Franklin Watts 2004
ISBN 978 0 7496 5576 1

Series editor: Sally Luck
Art Director: Jonathan Hair
Design: Rachel Hamdi/Holly Mann
Picture Research: Diana Morris

A CIP catalogue record for this book is available
from the British Library.

Every attempt has been made to clear copyright. Should there
be any inadvertent omission, please apply to
the publisher for rectification.

Printed in China

Franklin Watts is a division of Hachette Children's Books

Contents

London

London is the capital city of England. Its busy streets are full of people and traffic.

London Bridge

St Paul's Cathedral

The River Thames

Tower of London

△ London today

Have you been to a big city?
Did you see old and new buildings?
What did you hear and smell?

About 350 years ago, in 1666, London was much smaller. The streets were narrow, crowded and dirty. Many Londoners had died of a terrible plague. Another disaster was about to happen – the Great Fire of London.

The River Thames

St Paul's Cathedral

London Bridge

Tower of London

LONDRES

△ London in 1666

Be a historian...

Look carefully at the two pictures of London.

- What is different about them?
- What is the same?

Buildings

In 1666, houses in London were built of different materials from modern houses.

Thatch

Plaster

Wooden beams

Find out what was used to build your home. Do you think a 1660s house would catch fire more easily than a modern one?

At night, houses were lit with candles.
Flaming torches lit up the streets.
Open fires were used for
cooking and keeping warm.

Open fire

Burning candle

Modern cooker

Electric light

Be a historian...

- Which of these would you find in a 1660s house?
- Which would you find in a modern house?
- Which are safer to use? Can you say why?

The Great Fire starts

The fire started on 2nd September 1666.
Thomas Farynor, a baker, forgot to check
his oven before he went to sleep. Sparks
flew out and set fire to a pile of wood.

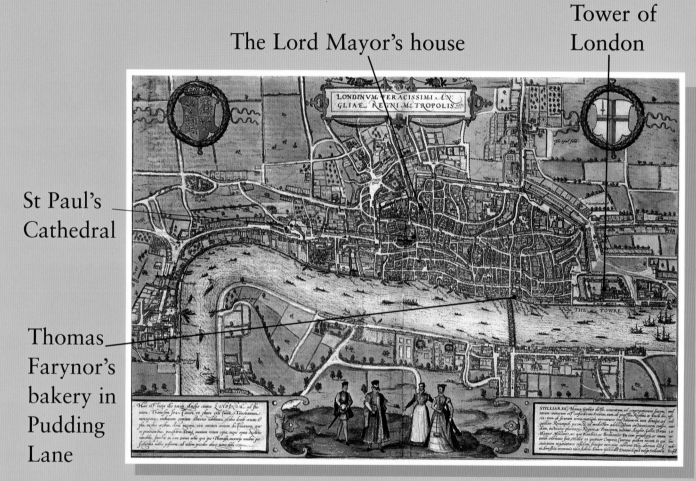

Tower of London

The Lord Mayor's house

St Paul's Cathedral

Thomas Farynor's bakery in Pudding Lane

Map of London in 1666

The summer had been hot and dry.
A warm east wind was blowing. The wood
burned quickly and the fire spread.

The fire woke the Lord Mayor of London but he went back to sleep. He thought there was nothing to worry about, but he was wrong...

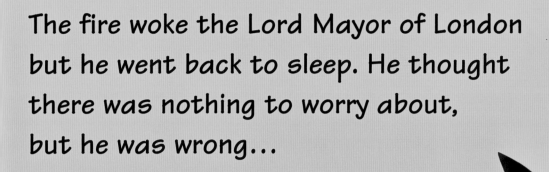

Be a historian...

Look back at pages 7–10. What clues can you find to tell you why the fire spread so quickly?

Talk about...

...what a fire would look, sound, feel and smell like.

Use these words to help you:

flames   sparks
smoke   crackling
burning   hot

Eyewitness

Samuel Pepys worked in an office near the Tower of London. He wrote in his diary every day, about life in London.

△ A page from Samuel Pepys's diary. He wrote in a special code.

△ Samuel Pepys

Pepys was an eyewitness to the Fire of London. That means he saw it happen. Pepys wrote about the fire in his diary.

Why is it *a good idea* to write about something you see the same day it happens?

You can be an eyewitness to all kinds of events, big or small. If you see something happen – you're an eyewitness.

There was a fire alarm at school today.

🔍 Be a historian...

Eyewitnesses can record what they have seen in lots of different ways, apart from writing.

- How else could you record an event?
- How else could Samuel Pepys have recorded what he saw?

Imagine you are Samuel Pepys, watching the fire from the Tower of London. What do you think he saw? Turn the page to find out...

The fire spreads

Pepys watched the fire from a safe place.

"I ... walked to the Tower ... and there I did see the houses at the end of the bridge all on fire ... everybody endeavouring to remove their goods, and flinging (them) into the river ..."

Escaping the fire by boat △

Why do you think people jumped into boats?

Imagine you were in one of the boats.

What would you see ? How would you feel?

The story of the fire filled the pages of the newspaper, *The London Gazette.*

"*...there hapned to break out, a sad in deplorable Fire in Pudding-lane ... This lamentable Fire in a short time became too big to be mastred by any Engines ... a violent and Easterly wind tormented it and kept it burning...*"

THE LONDON GAZETTE.

Published by Authority.

From Monday, Septemb 3, to Monday, Septemp 10, 1666.

Whitehall, Sept. 8.

THE ordinary course of this paper having been interrupted by a sad and lamentable accident of Fire lately hapned in the City of *London* : it hath been thought fit for satisfying the minds of so many of His Majesties good Subjects who must needs be concerned for the Issue of so great an accident, to give this short, but true Accompt of it.

On the second instant, at one of the clock in the Morning, there hapned to break out, a sad in deplorable Fire in *Pudding-lane*, neer *New Fish-street*, which falling out at that hour of the night, and in a quarter of the Town so close built with wooden pitched houses spread itself so far before day, and with such distraction to the inhabitants and Neighbours, that care was not taken for the timely preventing the further diffusion of it, by pulling down houses, as ought to have been ; so that this lamentable Fire in a short time became too big to be mastred by any Engines or working neer it. It fell out most unhappily too, That a violent Easterly wind fomented it, and kept it burning all that day, and the night following spreading itself up to *Grace-church-street* and downwards from *Cannon-street* to the Water-side, as far as the Three Cranes in the *Vintrey.*

The people in all parts about it, distracted by the vastness of it, and their particular care to carry away their Goods, many attempts were made to prevent the spreading of it by pulling down Houses, and making great Intervals, but all in vain, the Fire seizing upon the Timber and Rubbish, and so continuing it set even through those spaces, and raging in a bright flame all Monday and Teusday, not withstanding His Majesties own, and His Royal Highness's indefatigable and personal pains to apply all possible remedies to prevent it, calling upon and helping the people with their Guards ; and a great number of Nobility and Gentry unwearidly assisting therein, for which they were requited with a thousand blessings from the poor distressed people. By the favour of God the Wind slackened a little on Teusday night & the Flames meeting with brick buildings at the *Temple*, by little and little it was observed to lose its force on that side, so that on Wednesday morning we began to hope well, and his Royal

Church, neer *Holborn-bridge, Pie-corner, Aldersgate,* Cripple-gate, neer the lower end of *Coleman-street,* at the end of *Basin-hall-street* by the Postern at the upper end of *Bishopsgate-street* and *Leadenhall-street*, at the *Standard* in *Cornhill* at the church in Fenchurch street, neer *Cloth-workers Hall* in Minceing-*lane*, at the middle of *Mark-lane*, and at the Tower-dock.

On Thursday by the blessing of God it was wholly beat down and extinguished. But so as that Evening it unhappily burst out again a fresh at the *Temple*, by the falling of some sparks (as it supposed) upon a Pile of Wooden buildings ; but his Royal Highness who watched there that vvhole night in Person, by the great labours and diligence used, and especially by applying Powder to blow up the Houses about it, before day most happily mastered it.

Divers Strangers, Dutch and French were, during the fire, apprehended, upon suspicion that they contributed mischievously to it, who are all imprisoned, and Informations prepared to make a severe inquisition here upon by my Lord Chief Justice *Keeling*, assisted by some of the Lords of the Privy Council ; and some principal Members of the City, notwithstanding which suspicion, the manner of the burning all along in a Train, and so blowen forwards in all its way by strong Winds, make us conclude the whole was an effect of an unhappy chance, or to speak better, the heavy hand of God upon us for our sins, shewing us the terrour of his Judgement in thus raising the Fire and immediately after his miraculous and never be acknowledged Mercy, in putting a stop to when we were in the last despair, and that attempts for quenching it however industriou pursued seemed insufficient. His Majesty t sat hourly in Council, and ever since hath tinued making rounds about the City in all par it where the danger and mischief was greatest this morning that he hath sent his Grace the of *Albermarle*, whom he hath called for to him in this great occasion, to put his happ successful hand to the finishing this mem deliverance.

About the *Tower* the seasonable orders for plucking down the Houses to secure the zines of Powder was more especially su that part being up the Wind, notwith which it came almost to the very Gates o

Be a historian ...

- How can you tell this report was written a long time ago?
- Look at the front page of today's newspaper. How is it different from *The London Gazette?*

Fighting the fire

In 1666, people had to fight fires themselves with very simple tools.

◁ Firefighters in the 1600s used handsquirts and fire buckets made of leather.

The hand squirt only gave out one spray of water. ▽

Do you think these were useful tools to fight the Great Fire of London?

Where do you think the water came from?

How do people fight fires today?

Pepys went to the palace and warned King Charles II of the danger. The king, the Lord Mayor of London and Pepys himself all helped to put out the fire.

△ King Charles II

Modern firefighters △

Be a historian...

Look at the two pictures of firefighters.

- Do you think the firefighters in 1666 were well protected from the flames?
- Do modern firefighters' uniforms protect them?

What would you save?

Some people had time to save their precious possessions. Pepys saved his best wine and cheese from Italy. He buried them in his garden!

Some people saved their musical instruments.
▽

🔍 Be a historian...

- Why do you think cheese, wine and musical instruments were precious?
- If you could only save one of your possessions, which would you choose?

Some things are precious because they are worth a lot of money. Others are precious for different reasons.

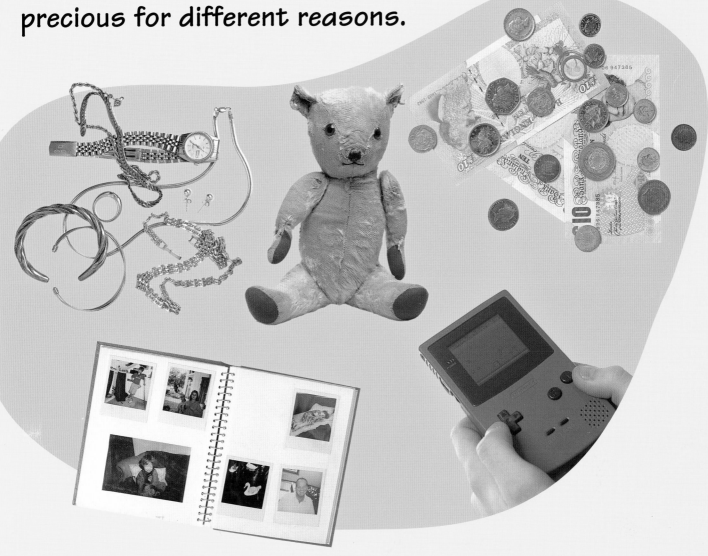

Which of these are precious because -
• they are worth a lot of money?
• they cannot be replaced?

After 3 days and 4 nights the fire died out. Can you guess what made this happen? Turn the page to find out...

The fire dies out

By Thursday 6th September, the wind had dropped and the fire died out. Only a small corner of the city of London had not been burnt down.

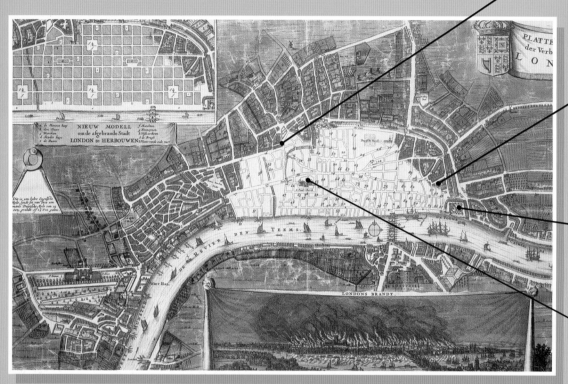

The fire ended at Pye Corner

Pepys's house (Navy Office)

Tower of London

Site of St Paul's Cathedral

Damage
- $4/5$ ths of the city of London burnt (white area on map)
- 87 churches burnt
- 13,000 houses burnt
- 6 people dead

Why do you think so few people died in the fire?

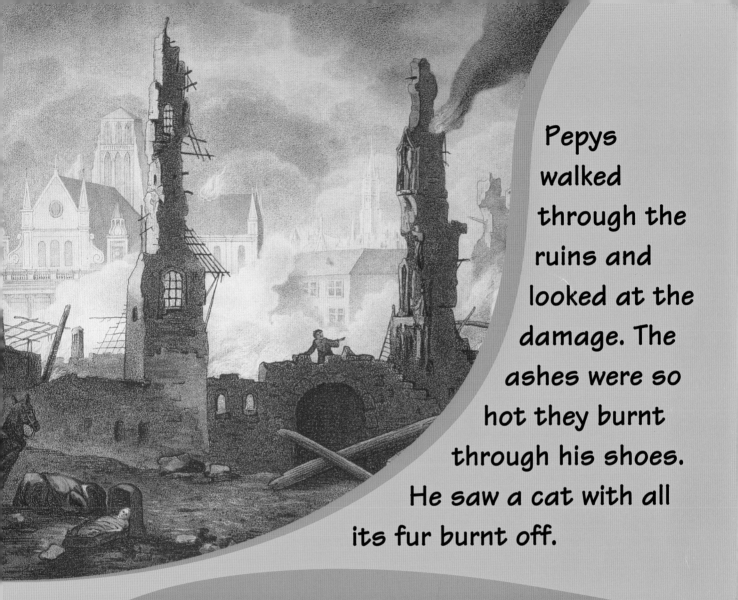

Pepys walked through the ruins and looked at the damage. The ashes were so hot they burnt through his shoes. He saw a cat with all its fur burnt off.

💬 Talk about...

. . . what it would be like to be in the burnt streets.

Use these words to help you:

sad	shocked	afraid
ruins	ashes	rubble

Can you imagine how the fire changed people's lives? Turn the page to find out...

Homeless

The fire left thousands of people homeless. Some were given shelter by people who still had homes. Others had to camp in fields.

Be a historian...

What help do you think the homeless people needed after the Great Fire of London?

Fires, earthquakes, floods and wars
are just some of the disasters that
can make people homeless. Today,
many people who have lost their
homes live in camps.

💬 Talk about...

... the different things that make people homeless.
What can you do to help people who have
lost their homes in a disaster?

Planning a new London

King Charles had great dreams of a new London. It would be like Paris, in France, and have grand stone buildings, wide avenues and green parks.

Prosp: de l'Hostel de Liancourt

A street in Paris in the 1600s

Be a historian...

Look back at page 7.

In what ways was Paris different from London?

Why did the king want London to be like Paris?

No one wanted such a terrible fire to happen again. New rules were made to stop London from burning so easily.

Rules

- Buildings must be made of brick and stone
- Streets must be wider and houses further apart
- Houses must be no more than four storeys high

How would these new rules help to save London from another fire?

Who do you think the king needed to help him carry out his plans? Turn the page to find out...

The King looks at plans for re-building London

A new city

The king needed an architect to draw up plans for re-building London. He chose Sir Christopher Wren.

△ Sir Christopher Wren

◁ Wren's plans for St Paul's Cathedral

Wren was put in charge of re-building St Paul's Cathedral and 51 other churches.

Many buildings were not built in the way that the king wanted. There was not enough money, and people wanted their new homes very quickly.

Some of Wren's plans were carried out. Buildings like St Paul's can still be seen in London today.

St Paul's
Cathedral today ▷

Be a historian...

Go to London and visit St Paul's Cathedral.
Visit Monument near Pudding Lane.
Sir Christopher Wren built it in memory
of the Great Fire of London.

Timeline

1665
Thousands of Londoners die of the plague.

1666
The summer in London is hot and dry.

Start

September 2nd
Fire starts in a bakery in Pudding Lane. Wind spreads the fire.

September 3rd
London is on fire. London Bridge burns down.

September 4th
The fire burns fiercely. St Paul's Cathedral burns down.

September 5th
King Charles II, the Lord Mayor and Samuel Pepys help to fight the fire.

September 6th
The fire goes out. Thousands of Londoners are homeless.

1669
Christopher Wren is chosen to plan a new city.

1675
Re-building St Paul's Cathedral begins.

End

1711
St Paul's Cathedral is finished.

Glossary

Architect
Someone who plans and designs buildings.

Diary
A book where you write about the things that happen to you each day.

Disaster
Something that causes terrible damage such as a fire or an earthquake.

Eyewitness
Someone who sees something happening with their own eyes.

Materials
What things are made of, such as bricks, wood and plaster.

Plague
A disease that is passed very easily from person to person. Plagues killed many people.

Possessions
The things that people own.

Report
A written account of something that has happened.

Ruins
What is left of a building when it has been burnt or damaged.

Index